# Will and Estate Planning

Laurel D. Malvern

Copyright © 2024 by Laurel D. Malvern

All rights reserved. No part of this book may be reproduced, distributed, or transmitted in any form or by any means, including photocopying, recording, or other electronic or mechanical methods, without the prior written permission of the publisher, except in the case of brief quotations embodied in critical reviews and certain other noncommercial uses permitted by copyright law.

This book is intended to provide general information and guidance on the topic of will and estate planning. The author, Laurel D. Malvern, is not engaged in rendering legal, financial, or professional services. The information contained herein is based on the author's personal experience, research, and understanding of the subject matter, and it should not be considered a substitute for professional advice. Readers are encouraged to consult with qualified legal and financial professionals regarding their specific circumstances and to obtain personalized guidance tailored to their needs.

While every effort has been made to ensure the accuracy and completeness of the information presented in this book, the author and the publisher assume no responsibility for errors, inaccuracies, or omissions. The author and the publisher shall have no liability for any damages, losses, or injuries arising from the use of or reliance on the information provided herein.

Trademarked names, logos, and images mentioned in this book are the property of their respective owners and are used for identification purposes only. Such use does not imply endorsement or affiliation with the book or its author.

Any references to specific products, services, or organizations are provided for informational purposes only and do not constitute an endorsement or recommendation by the author or the publisher.

"Will and Estate Planning"

*Preface 8*

*Chapter 1: Setting the Stage: Understanding the Importance of Will and Estate Planning 10*

*Chapter 2: Defining Key Concepts: Wills, Trusts, and Probate 12*

*Chapter 3: Assessing Your Assets and Liabilities: Taking Stock of Your Estate 14*

*Chapter 4: Identifying Your Objectives: What Do You Want Your Legacy to Be? 16*

*Chapter 5: Crafting Your Will 19*

*Chapter 6: The Anatomy of a Will: Essential Components and Legal Requirements 21*

*Chapter 7: Choosing Your Beneficiaries: Determining Who Will Inherit Your Assets 24*

*Chapter 8: Appointing Executors and Guardians: Entrusting Key Responsibilities 27*

*Chapter 9: Understanding Legal Formalities: Signing and Executing Your Will Properly 31*

*Chapter 10: Exploring Trusts and Other Estate Planning Tools 34*

*Chapter 11: Understanding Trusts: Types, Benefits, and Considerations 37*

*Chapter 12: Special Considerations for Complex Assets: Real Estate, Businesses, and Investments 41*

*Chapter 13: Utilizing Powers of Attorney and Advance Directives: Ensuring Decision-Making in Times of Incapacity 45*

*Chapter 14: Charitable Giving Strategies: Leaving a Lasting Impact Through Philanthropy 49*

*Chapter 15: Strategies for Minimizing Taxes and Maximizing Benefits 53*

*Chapter 16: Navigating Estate Taxes: Understanding Your Obligations and Opportunities 57*

*Chapter 17: Leveraging Tax-Advantaged Accounts: IRAs, 401(k)s, and Other Retirement Vehicles 60*

*Chapter 18: Maximizing Social Security and Pension Benefits: Planning for Retirement Income Streams 64*

*Chapter 19: Addressing Family Dynamics and Potential Challenges 67*

*Chapter 20: Communicating Your Intentions: Discussing Your Estate Plan With Loved Ones 71*

*Chapter 21: Handling Blended Families and Complex Relationships: Strategies for Fair and Equitable Distribution 74*

*Chapter 22: Planning for Incapacity and End-of-Life Care: Health Care Directives and Medical Decision-Making 78*

*Chapter 23: Putting Your Plan Into Action 82*

*Chapter 24: Working With Legal Professionals: Finding the Right Estate Planning Attorney 85*

*Chapter 25: Conclusion 88*

*Glossary of Estate Planning Terms and Conditions 91*

*Estate Planning Checklist 93*

*Here's a basic template for a simple will: 96*

# Preface

Welcome to "Will and Estate Planning: A Comprehensive Guide to Securing Your Legacy."

In today's rapidly changing world, it's easy to overlook the importance of planning for the future. Yet, as we navigate the complexities of life, it becomes increasingly clear that having a well-crafted estate plan is essential for ensuring that our wishes are carried out, our loved ones are provided for, and our legacy endures.

As an estate planning attorney with years of experience helping individuals and families navigate the intricacies of wills, trusts, and probate, I've witnessed firsthand the transformative power of proactive planning. In this book, I aim to demystify the process of estate planning and empower you to take control of your financial future with confidence and clarity.

Whether you're just beginning to explore the world of estate planning or you're seeking to update an existing plan, this book is designed to serve as your trusted companion on the journey ahead. Through a combination of practical advice, real-life examples, and expert insights, I'll guide you step-by-step through the process of creating a customized estate plan that reflects your unique goals, values, and priorities.

From understanding the basics of wills and trusts to navigating complex tax considerations and family dynamics, each chapter is crafted to provide you with the knowledge and tools you need to make informed decisions and protect what matters most. Along the way, I'll address common misconceptions, dispel myths, and offer tips for overcoming potential challenges.

Above all, my goal is to empower you to embrace the peace of mind that comes from knowing your affairs are in order and your loved ones are provided for. By taking proactive steps today, you can ensure that your legacy will endure for generations to come.

Thank you for embarking on this journey with me. I hope that this book will serve as a valuable resource and guide as you navigate the exciting and rewarding process of will and estate planning.

**Warm regards,**

**Laurel D. Malvern**

# Chapter 1: Setting the Stage: Understanding the Importance of Will and Estate Planning

Introduction:

Welcome to the first chapter of "Will and Estate Planning." In this chapter, we'll delve into the fundamental importance of will and estate planning. We'll explore why these processes are essential for individuals and families, regardless of their age, income level, or family dynamics. By the end of this chapter, you'll have a clear understanding of why creating an estate plan is a crucial step in safeguarding your assets and ensuring your wishes are carried out.

Why Estate Planning Matters:

Estate planning is often misunderstood or overlooked, yet its significance cannot be overstated. At its core, estate planning is about much more than just distributing assets after death. It's about protecting your loved ones, minimizing taxes, and preserving your legacy for future generations. Without a comprehensive estate plan in place, your assets may be subject to unnecessary taxes and probate costs, and your loved ones may face unnecessary stress and uncertainty during an already difficult time.

Key Concepts:

In this section, we'll define key concepts related to estate planning, including wills, trusts, and probate. We'll discuss the role of each component in the estate planning process and explain how they work together to achieve your goals. By understanding these fundamental concepts, you'll be better equipped to make informed decisions about your estate plan.

The Consequences of Not Having a Plan:

Many individuals put off estate planning, assuming that it's something they can address later in life. However, the reality is that none of us are guaranteed tomorrow. Without a plan in place, your assets may be distributed according to state intestacy laws, which may not align with your wishes. Moreover, without clear instructions, family disputes and legal challenges may arise, leading to unnecessary conflict and expense.

Conclusion:

As we conclude this chapter, I encourage you to reflect on the importance of will and estate planning in your own life. Regardless of your age or financial situation, creating an estate plan is a proactive step that can provide peace of mind and protect your loved ones. In the chapters that follow, we'll delve deeper into the estate planning process and provide you with the tools and knowledge you need to create a comprehensive plan that reflects your unique goals and values.

# Chapter 2: Defining Key Concepts: Wills, Trusts, and Probate

Welcome to Chapter 2 of "Will and Estate Planning." In this chapter, we'll delve into the key concepts that form the foundation of estate planning: wills, trusts, and probate. Understanding these fundamental concepts is essential for navigating the estate planning process and ensuring that your wishes are carried out effectively.

Wills:

A will is a legal document that allows you to specify how you want your assets to be distributed after your death. In your will, you can name beneficiaries to receive specific assets, appoint an executor to oversee the distribution of your estate, and designate guardians for minor children. Wills provide a clear and legally enforceable framework for distributing your assets and ensuring that your wishes are carried out according to your instructions.

Trusts:

A trust is a legal arrangement in which one party (the trustee) holds assets on behalf of another party (the beneficiary). Trusts can be used for a variety of purposes, including asset protection, tax planning, and ensuring the smooth transfer of assets to beneficiaries. Unlike wills, which only take effect after death, trusts can be established during your lifetime and can provide flexibility and control over the distribution of your assets both during your lifetime and after your death.

Probate:

Probate is the legal process through which a deceased person's estate is administered and distributed. During probate, the court oversees the validation of the will, the identification and appraisal of assets, the payment of debts and taxes, and the distribution of remaining assets to beneficiaries. While probate serves an important purpose in ensuring that a deceased person's wishes are carried out and that creditors are paid, it can also be time-consuming, costly, and public. Understanding the probate process and its implications is essential for effective estate planning.

Conclusion:

As we conclude this chapter, I encourage you to reflect on the key concepts of wills, trusts, and probate and consider how they apply to your own estate planning goals. By understanding these fundamental concepts, you'll be better equipped to make informed decisions and create a comprehensive estate plan that protects your assets, provides for your loved ones, and ensures that your wishes are carried out according to your instructions. In the chapters that follow, we'll delve deeper into the estate planning process and provide you with the tools and knowledge you need to create a plan that reflects your unique goals and values.

# Chapter 3: Assessing Your Assets and Liabilities: Taking Stock of Your Estate

Welcome to Chapter 3 of "Will and Estate Planning." In this chapter, we'll explore the crucial step of assessing your assets and liabilities as part of the estate planning process. By taking stock of your financial holdings and obligations, you'll gain a clear understanding of your estate's value and be better equipped to develop a comprehensive plan that protects your assets and achieves your goals.

Inventory of Assets:

The first step in assessing your estate is to compile a thorough inventory of your assets. This includes identifying all of your financial holdings, such as bank accounts, investments, retirement accounts, and life insurance policies. It also involves cataloging your tangible assets, such as real estate, vehicles, jewelry, and valuable personal property. By creating a comprehensive list of your assets, you'll have a clear picture of your estate's total value and be able to make informed decisions about how to distribute your assets effectively.

Evaluation of Liabilities:

In addition to identifying your assets, it's essential to assess your liabilities as part of the estate planning process. This includes accounting for any debts you owe, such as mortgages, loans, credit card balances, and outstanding bills. Understanding your liabilities is crucial for determining your net worth and ensuring that your estate has sufficient liquidity to cover any outstanding debts and expenses. By evaluating your liabilities alongside your assets, you'll be better prepared to create a plan that protects your estate and minimizes the impact of taxes and other financial obligations.

Consideration of Special Assets:

Some assets may require special consideration during the estate planning process. For example, if you own a business, you'll need to assess its value and determine how it fits into your overall estate plan. Similarly, if you have assets held in trusts or other complex structures, you'll need to understand how these assets are managed and distributed. By considering the unique characteristics of these special assets, you can ensure that they are properly accounted for and integrated into your estate plan in a way that aligns with your goals and objectives.

Conclusion:

As we conclude this chapter, I encourage you to take the time to assess your assets and liabilities carefully. By gaining a clear understanding of your financial situation, you'll be better equipped to develop a comprehensive estate plan that protects your assets, provides for your loved ones, and achieves your long-term objectives. In the chapters that follow, we'll continue to explore key aspects of the estate planning process and provide you with the knowledge and tools you need to create a plan that reflects your unique circumstances and priorities.

# Chapter 4: Identifying Your Objectives: What Do You Want Your Legacy to Be?

Welcome to Chapter 4 of "Will and Estate Planning." In this chapter, we'll delve into the essential step of identifying your objectives in the estate planning process. By clarifying your goals and priorities, you'll be better equipped to create a plan that reflects your values, provides for your loved ones, and ensures that your legacy endures for generations to come.

Defining Your Legacy:

Your legacy is more than just the sum of your assets. It encompasses the values, principles, and memories that you leave behind for your loved ones and future generations. In this section, we'll explore what legacy means to you and how you envision it shaping the lives of those you care about. By defining your legacy, you'll gain clarity on your estate planning objectives and be better prepared to create a plan that aligns with your vision for the future.

Providing for Your Loved Ones:

One of the primary objectives of estate planning is to provide for the financial security and well-being of your loved ones after you're gone. In this section, we'll discuss how to identify the needs of your family members and ensure that they are adequately provided for in your estate plan. Whether you're supporting a spouse, children, grandchildren, or other dependents, understanding their financial needs and aspirations is essential for creating a plan that protects their interests and preserves your legacy.

Supporting Charitable Causes:

Many individuals choose to include charitable giving as part of their estate plan as a way to give back to their community and support causes they care about. In this section, we'll explore how to identify charitable organizations and causes that align with your values and objectives. Whether you're passionate about education, healthcare, the environment, or social justice, incorporating charitable giving into your estate plan can be a meaningful way to leave a lasting impact and create a positive legacy for future generations.

Minimizing Tax Liabilities:

Another key objective of estate planning is to minimize tax liabilities and maximize the value of your estate for your beneficiaries. In this section, we'll discuss common estate tax planning strategies and how to structure your estate to take advantage of available tax exemptions and deductions. By understanding the tax implications of your estate plan, you can ensure that more of your assets are passed on to your loved ones and less is lost to taxes and other expenses.

Conclusion:

As we conclude this chapter, I encourage you to reflect on your objectives in the estate planning process and consider how they align with your values and priorities. By identifying your goals and aspirations, you'll be better equipped to create a comprehensive estate plan that protects your assets, provides for your loved ones, and leaves a meaningful legacy for future generations. In the chapters that follow, we'll continue to explore key aspects of the estate planning process and provide you with the knowledge and tools you need to achieve your estate planning objectives.

# Chapter 5: Crafting Your Will

Welcome to Chapter 5 of "Will and Estate Planning." In this pivotal chapter, we'll dive into the process of crafting your last will and testament, a cornerstone of your estate plan. Your will is a powerful legal document that allows you to specify how you want your assets to be distributed after your death and to make important decisions about the guardianship of your minor children, among other things. By understanding the key components and considerations of a will, you'll be able to create a document that reflects your wishes and provides clarity for your loved ones.

Understanding the Purpose of Your Will:

Your will serves as a roadmap for the distribution of your assets and the fulfillment of your wishes after your passing. In this section, we'll explore the primary purposes of a will, including naming beneficiaries, appointing an executor, and specifying guardians for minor children. We'll also discuss how your will fits into the broader context of your estate plan and the importance of coordinating it with other estate planning documents, such as trusts and advance directives.

Key Components of Your Will:

A well-crafted will contains several key components that are essential for ensuring its validity and effectiveness. In this section, we'll discuss these components in detail, including:

Identification of the Testator: Your will should begin with a clear statement identifying you as the testator, along with your full legal name and place of residence.

Appointment of Executor: Your will allows you to appoint an executor, who is responsible for carrying out your wishes and administering your estate after your death.

Bequests and Distributions: Your will enables you to specify how you want your assets to be distributed among your beneficiaries, whether they are family members, friends, or charitable organizations.

Residuary Clause: This clause addresses any assets that are not specifically mentioned in your will and ensures that they are distributed according to your wishes.

Guardianship Provisions: If you have minor children, your will allows you to designate guardians who will care for them in the event of your death.

Execution and Formalities:

In this section, we'll discuss the legal formalities required for the execution of your will, including the witnessing, and signing requirements. We'll also address common mistakes to avoid when drafting your will, such as failing to update it regularly or neglecting to consider potential challenges to its validity.

Conclusion:

As we conclude this chapter, I encourage you to reflect on the importance of crafting a will as part of your estate plan. By understanding the key components and considerations of a will, you'll be better equipped to create a document that accurately reflects your wishes and provides clarity for your loved ones. In the chapters that follow, we'll continue to explore other important aspects of the estate planning process and provide you with the knowledge and tools you need to create a comprehensive plan that protects your assets and provides for your loved ones.

# Chapter 6: The Anatomy of a Will: Essential Components and Legal Requirements

Welcome to Chapter 6 of "Will and Estate Planning." In this chapter, we'll dissect the anatomy of a will, exploring its essential components and the legal requirements necessary for its validity. Understanding the structure and content of a will is crucial for ensuring that your wishes are accurately reflected and legally enforceable. By familiarizing yourself with the key elements of a will, you'll be better prepared to craft a document that effectively communicates your intentions and provides clarity for your loved ones.

Essential Components of a Will:

A well-drafted will contains several essential components that serve to clarify your intentions and provide guidance for the distribution of your assets. In this section, we'll explore these components in detail, including:

Introduction: Your will should begin with an introductory statement identifying you as the testator and revoking any previous wills or codicils.
Appointment of Executor: You'll designate an executor, who is responsible for administering your estate and carrying out the instructions outlined in your will.

Bequests and Distributions: Your will specifies how you want your assets to be distributed among your beneficiaries, whether they are individuals, organizations, or charities.
Residuary Clause: This clause addresses any assets not specifically mentioned in your will and ensures that they are distributed according to your wishes.
Contingency Plans: Your will may include contingency plans to address various scenarios, such as the death of a beneficiary or the inability of your chosen executor to serve.
Guardianship Provisions: If you have minor children, your will allows you to designate guardians who will care for them in the event of your death.
Legal Requirements for Validity:

In addition to including the necessary components, your will must meet certain legal requirements to be valid and enforceable. These requirements vary depending on state law but generally include:

Testamentary Capacity: You must be of sound mind and legal age to create a will, meaning that you understand the nature and consequences of your decisions.
Voluntariness: Your will must be executed voluntarily, without coercion or undue influence from others.
Formalities: Your will must be executed in accordance with the formalities prescribed by state law, which typically include witnessing and signing requirements.
No Revocation: Your will must not have been revoked or superseded by a subsequent will or codicil.
Conclusion:

As we conclude this chapter, I encourage you to consider the essential components and legal requirements of a will as you embark on the estate planning process. By understanding the structure and content of a will, you'll be better equipped to craft a document that accurately reflects your wishes and provides peace of mind for you and your loved ones. In the chapters that follow, we'll continue to explore other important aspects of the estate planning process and provide you with the knowledge and tools you need to create a comprehensive plan that protects your assets and provides for your legacy.

# Chapter 7: Choosing Your Beneficiaries: Determining Who Will Inherit Your Assets

Welcome to Chapter 7 of "Will and Estate Planning." In this chapter, we'll explore the critical decision of choosing your beneficiaries—the individuals or entities who will inherit your assets after your passing. Selecting beneficiaries is one of the most significant aspects of estate planning, as it directly impacts the distribution of your wealth and the fulfillment of your wishes. By carefully considering your options and understanding the implications of your choices, you can create a plan that reflects your values and provides for your loved ones in a meaningful way.

Identifying Potential Beneficiaries:

The first step in choosing your beneficiaries is to identify the individuals or entities you wish to include in your estate plan. This may include family members, friends, charitable organizations, or other entities. In this section, we'll discuss factors to consider when selecting beneficiaries, such as your relationship with them, their financial needs, and their ability to manage inheritance responsibly. We'll also explore how to address complex family dynamics and ensure that your estate plan reflects your intentions accurately.

Providing for Loved Ones:

One of the primary objectives of estate planning is to provide for the financial security and well-being of your loved ones after your passing. In this section, we'll discuss strategies for providing for your beneficiaries in a way that meets their needs and supports their long-term goals. Whether you're supporting a spouse, children, grandchildren, or other dependents, understanding their unique circumstances and aspirations is essential for creating a plan that protects their interests and preserves your legacy.

Supporting Charitable Causes:

Many individuals choose to include charitable organizations as beneficiaries in their estate plans as a way to give back to their communities and support causes they care about. In this section, we'll explore the benefits of incorporating charitable giving into your estate plan and discuss strategies for maximizing the impact of your charitable contributions. Whether you're passionate about education, healthcare, the environment, or social justice, leaving a legacy of philanthropy can be a meaningful way to make a positive impact on the world.

Addressing Special Considerations:

Some beneficiaries may require special consideration in your estate plan, such as individuals with disabilities, minor children, or beneficiaries with financial challenges. In this section, we'll discuss strategies for addressing these special considerations and ensuring that your estate plan provides for their needs in a responsible and compassionate manner. We'll also explore tools such as special needs trusts and minor's trusts that can help protect vulnerable beneficiaries and preserve their eligibility for government benefits.

Conclusion:

As we conclude this chapter, I encourage you to reflect on the important decision of choosing your beneficiaries and consider how it aligns with your values and priorities. By thoughtfully selecting your beneficiaries and providing for their needs in a meaningful way, you can create a legacy that reflects your generosity and compassion. In the chapters that follow, we'll continue to explore other critical aspects of the estate planning process and provide you with the knowledge and tools you need to create a comprehensive plan that protects your assets and provides for your loved ones.

# Chapter 8: Appointing Executors and Guardians: Entrusting Key Responsibilities

Welcome to Chapter 8 of "Will and Estate Planning." In this chapter, we'll delve into the crucial decisions of appointing executors and guardians in your estate plan. Executors play a pivotal role in administering your estate and ensuring that your wishes are carried out, while guardians are responsible for caring for your minor children in the event of your passing. By carefully selecting individuals who are trustworthy, competent, and aligned with your values, you can entrust these key responsibilities with confidence and peace of mind.

Appointing Executors:

An executor is responsible for managing the administration of your estate after your passing, including gathering and inventorying assets, paying debts and taxes, and distributing assets to beneficiaries according to your wishes. In this section, we'll discuss factors to consider when selecting an executor, such as their trustworthiness, organizational skills, and willingness to serve. We'll also explore the importance of communicating your expectations clearly with your chosen executor and ensuring that they understand their duties and responsibilities.

Choosing Guardians for Minor Children:

If you have minor children, appointing guardians is one of the most critical decisions you'll make in your estate plan. Guardians are responsible for providing care and support for your children in the event of your passing, ensuring that their physical, emotional, and financial needs are met. In this section, we'll discuss factors to consider when selecting guardians, such as their parenting style, values, and ability to provide a stable and loving environment for your children. We'll also explore the importance of discussing your wishes with potential guardians and ensuring that they are willing and able to accept the responsibility.

Coordinating Responsibilities:

In some cases, you may choose to appoint the same individual or individuals to serve as both executor and guardian in your estate plan. In this section, we'll discuss the benefits and considerations of combining these roles and how to ensure effective coordination between them. We'll also explore strategies for addressing potential conflicts of interest and ensuring that the best interests of your estate and your children are prioritized.

Succession Planning for Executors and Guardians:

It's essential to include provisions for succession planning in your estate plan to address situations where your chosen executor or guardian is unable or unwilling to serve. In this section, we'll discuss strategies for appointing alternate executors and guardians and ensuring that your estate plan remains flexible and adaptable to changing circumstances.

Conclusion:

As we conclude this chapter, I encourage you to reflect on the important decisions of appointing executors and guardians in your estate plan and consider how they align with your values and priorities. By carefully selecting individuals who are trustworthy, competent, and aligned with your wishes, you can entrust these key responsibilities with confidence and peace of mind. In the chapters that follow, we'll continue to explore other critical aspects of the estate planning process and provide you with the knowledge and tools you need to create a comprehensive plan that protects your assets and provides for your loved ones.

# Chapter 9: Understanding Legal Formalities: Signing and Executing Your Will Properly

Welcome to Chapter 9 of "Will and Estate Planning." In this chapter, we'll explore the critical legal formalities involved in signing and executing your will properly. While creating a will is a significant step in the estate planning process, it's essential to ensure that your document meets all legal requirements to be valid and enforceable. By understanding the necessary formalities and taking the proper steps to execute your will, you can protect your wishes and provide clarity for your loved ones.

Legal Requirements for Signing Your Will:

In order for your will to be valid and legally enforceable, it must meet certain legal requirements for signing and execution. These requirements vary depending on state law but generally include:

Testamentary Capacity: You must be of sound mind and legal age to create a will, meaning that you understand the nature and consequences of your decisions.
Voluntariness: Your will must be executed voluntarily, without coercion or undue influence from others.

Witnessing: Your will must be signed in the presence of witnesses who can attest to your mental capacity and the voluntariness of your actions. The number of witnesses required varies by state but typically ranges from two to three.
Signature: You must sign your will at the end of the document to indicate that it reflects your wishes and intentions.
Ensuring Proper Execution:

In addition to meeting the legal requirements for signing your will, it's essential to take certain steps to ensure that the execution process is conducted properly. In this section, we'll discuss best practices for executing your will, including:

Choosing Witnesses: Select witnesses who are of legal age, competent, and not named as beneficiaries in your will. Witnesses should also be impartial and have no conflicts of interest.
Signing in the Presence of Witnesses: Sign your will in the presence of your witnesses, and ensure that they sign the document as well. Witnesses should observe each other's signatures to confirm that the document has been properly executed.
Acknowledgment: After signing your will, you may choose to acknowledge your signature in front of a notary public to further validate the document's authenticity.
Storing and Safeguarding Your Will:

Once your will has been properly executed, it's crucial to store and safeguard the document in a secure location. In this section, we'll discuss strategies for storing your will safely, such as keeping it in a fireproof safe or depositing it with a trusted individual or institution. We'll also explore the importance of informing your executor and loved ones of the location of your will and ensuring that they have access to it when needed.

Conclusion:

As we conclude this chapter, I encourage you to familiarize yourself with the legal formalities involved in signing and executing your will properly. By understanding these requirements and taking the necessary steps to ensure proper execution, you can protect your wishes and provide clarity for your loved ones. In the chapters that follow, we'll continue to explore other critical aspects of the estate planning process and provide you with the knowledge and tools you need to create a comprehensive plan that protects your assets and provides for your legacy.

# Chapter 10: Exploring Trusts and Other Estate Planning Tools

Welcome to Chapter 10 of "Will and Estate Planning." In this chapter, we'll explore trusts and other estate planning tools that can complement your will and help you achieve your long-term financial goals. While wills are a foundational component of estate planning, trusts offer additional flexibility, control, and protection for your assets. By understanding the various types of trusts and other estate planning tools available, you can create a comprehensive plan that addresses your unique needs and objectives.

Understanding Trusts:

A trust is a legal arrangement in which one party (the trustee) holds assets on behalf of another party (the beneficiary). Trusts can be used for a variety of purposes, including asset protection, tax planning, and ensuring the smooth transfer of assets to beneficiaries. In this section, we'll explore the different types of trusts, including revocable trusts, irrevocable trusts, and special needs trusts, and discuss how they can be used to achieve specific estate planning goals.

Maximizing Tax Efficiency:

One of the primary benefits of trusts is their ability to minimize tax liabilities and maximize the value of your estate for your beneficiaries. In this section, we'll discuss common tax planning strategies using trusts, such as bypass trusts, charitable remainder trusts, and generation-skipping trusts. We'll also explore how trusts can be used to take advantage of available tax exemptions and deductions, such as the estate tax exemption and the gift tax annual exclusion.

Protecting Assets:

Trusts can also provide valuable asset protection benefits by shielding your assets from creditors, lawsuits, and other potential threats. In this section, we'll discuss how certain types of trusts, such as irrevocable trusts and asset protection trusts, can help safeguard your wealth and preserve it for future generations. We'll also explore strategies for structuring trusts to provide maximum protection while still maintaining flexibility and control over your assets.

Planning for Incapacity:

In addition to providing for the distribution of your assets after your passing, trusts can also be used to plan for incapacity and ensure that your financial affairs are managed effectively in the event that you become unable to make decisions for yourself. In this section, we'll discuss how revocable living trusts and durable powers of attorney can be used to appoint trusted individuals to manage your affairs and make decisions on your behalf if you become incapacitated.

Conclusion:

As we conclude this chapter, I encourage you to explore the various trusts and other estate planning tools available and consider how they may complement your existing estate plan. By understanding the benefits and considerations of each option, you can create a comprehensive plan that protects your assets, minimizes tax liabilities, and provides for your loved ones in a meaningful way. In the chapters that follow, we'll continue to explore other critical aspects of the estate planning process and provide you with the knowledge and tools you need to achieve your estate planning objectives.

# Chapter 11: Understanding Trusts: Types, Benefits, and Considerations

Welcome to Chapter 11 of "Will and Estate Planning." In this chapter, we'll delve deeper into trusts, exploring their various types, benefits, and important considerations. Trusts are powerful estate planning tools that offer flexibility, control, and protection for your assets. By understanding the different types of trusts available and their potential benefits and considerations, you can make informed decisions about incorporating trusts into your estate plan to achieve your long-term financial goals.

Types of Trusts:

Trusts come in many forms, each designed to serve specific purposes and achieve different objectives. In this section, we'll explore some common types of trusts, including:

Revocable Living Trusts: These trusts are established during your lifetime and can be modified or revoked at any time. They are often used to avoid probate, provide for incapacity planning, and maintain privacy in the estate administration process.
Irrevocable Trusts: Irrevocable trusts cannot be modified or revoked once established, making them more permanent in nature. They are commonly used for asset protection, tax planning, and Medicaid planning purposes.

Testamentary Trusts: These trusts are created through provisions in your will and only take effect after your death. They are often used to provide for minor children, individuals with special needs, or to implement tax planning strategies.

Special Needs Trusts: Also known as supplemental needs trusts, these trusts are designed to provide for individuals with disabilities without jeopardizing their eligibility for government benefits such as Medicaid and Supplemental Security Income (SSI).

Charitable Trusts: These trusts are established to support charitable causes and organizations while providing tax benefits for the donor. Common types of charitable trusts include charitable remainder trusts and charitable lead trusts.

Benefits of Trusts:

Trusts offer a range of benefits that make them valuable tools for estate planning. In this section, we'll explore some of the key benefits of trusts, including:

Probate Avoidance: Assets held in trusts typically bypass the probate process, resulting in faster and more efficient distribution to beneficiaries.

Privacy Protection: Unlike wills, which become public record upon probate, trusts allow for the private administration and distribution of assets without court oversight.

Asset Protection: Certain types of trusts, such as irrevocable trusts and asset protection trusts, can shield assets from creditors, lawsuits, and other potential threats.

Tax Efficiency: Trusts can be used to minimize estate taxes, gift taxes, and generation-skipping transfer taxes, allowing you to preserve more of your wealth for future generations.

Incapacity Planning: Revocable living trusts can provide for the management of your assets and affairs in the event of your incapacity, avoiding the need for court-appointed guardianship or conservatorship.

Considerations When Using Trusts:

While trusts offer many benefits, it's essential to consider certain factors and potential drawbacks when incorporating trusts into your estate plan. In this section, we'll discuss some important considerations, including:

Costs: Establishing and administering trusts can involve upfront costs and ongoing expenses, such as legal fees, trustee fees, and investment management fees.

Complexity: Trusts can be complex legal instruments that require careful planning and ongoing management. Working with experienced professionals, such as estate planning attorneys and financial advisors, can help ensure that your trusts are structured properly and achieve your intended objectives.

Loss of Control: Irrevocable trusts, in particular, involve relinquishing control over your assets, as you cannot modify or revoke the trust once established. It's essential to carefully consider the implications of transferring assets to an irrevocable trust and ensure that you are comfortable with the terms and conditions.

Legal and Tax Implications: Trusts are subject to various legal and tax rules, which can vary depending on state law and individual circumstances. It's crucial to work with knowledgeable professionals to understand the legal and tax implications of your trust planning and ensure compliance with applicable laws and regulations.

Conclusion:

As we conclude this chapter, I encourage you to explore the different types of trusts available and consider how they may fit into your estate planning goals. By understanding the benefits and considerations of trusts, you can make informed decisions about incorporating these powerful tools into your estate plan to achieve your long-term financial objectives. In the chapters that follow, we'll continue to explore other critical aspects of the estate planning process and provide you with the knowledge and tools you need to create a comprehensive plan that protects your assets and provides for your loved ones.

# Chapter 12: Special Considerations for Complex Assets: Real Estate, Businesses, and Investments

Welcome to Chapter 12 of "Will and Estate Planning." In this chapter, we'll explore special considerations for managing complex assets in your estate plan, focusing on real estate, businesses, and investments. These assets often require unique planning strategies to ensure their smooth transition to your beneficiaries and minimize potential challenges during the estate administration process. By understanding the specific considerations associated with these complex assets, you can develop a comprehensive estate plan that protects your legacy and provides for your loved ones effectively.

Real Estate:

Real estate is a significant asset for many individuals and may include primary residences, vacation homes, rental properties, and undeveloped land. In this section, we'll discuss special considerations for including real estate in your estate plan, including:

Property Ownership Structures: Choosing the right ownership structure for your real estate can impact how it is transferred to your beneficiaries and may have tax implications. Options include sole ownership, joint tenancy, tenancy in common, and ownership through trusts or other entities.

Property Valuation: Accurately valuing real estate is essential for estate tax purposes and ensuring that your beneficiaries receive their fair share of your estate. Professional appraisals can help determine the fair market value of your properties and avoid disputes among beneficiaries.

Mortgage and Debt Considerations: If your real estate is encumbered by mortgages or other debts, it's essential to consider how these obligations will be addressed in your estate plan. Strategies may include paying off debts using other assets, transferring ownership subject to existing liabilities, or establishing trusts to manage mortgage payments.

Business Interests:

Business interests, including ownership stakes in closely held businesses, partnerships, and corporate stock, present unique challenges in estate planning. In this section, we'll discuss special considerations for including business interests in your estate plan, including:

Succession Planning: Planning for the transfer of business ownership is crucial for ensuring continuity and preserving the value of your business. Options include transferring ownership to family members, key employees, or third-party buyers, or establishing buy-sell agreements among business partners.

Business Valuation: Accurately valuing business interests is essential for estate tax purposes and determining their fair value for distribution to beneficiaries. Professional business appraisals can help assess the value of your business and inform your estate planning decisions.

Business Structure and Entity Planning: The legal structure of your business can impact how it is transferred to your beneficiaries and may have tax implications. Options include sole proprietorships, partnerships, limited liability companies (LLCs), and corporations, each with its own advantages and considerations.

Investment Assets:

Investment assets, including stocks, bonds, mutual funds, and retirement accounts, play a significant role in many estate plans. In this section, we'll discuss special considerations for managing investment assets in your estate plan, including:

Beneficiary Designations: Many investment assets allow you to designate beneficiaries directly, bypassing probate and ensuring a smooth transfer of assets to your heirs. It's essential to review and update beneficiary designations regularly to reflect changes in your circumstances and ensure that your assets are distributed according to your wishes.

Tax Planning Strategies: Investment assets may be subject to capital gains taxes, income taxes, and estate taxes, depending on various factors such as the type of asset, its value, and how it is transferred to beneficiaries. Strategies for minimizing tax liabilities may include gifting assets during your lifetime, establishing trusts, or utilizing tax-deferred retirement accounts.

Investment Management: Proper investment management is essential for preserving and growing your assets over time. Working with experienced financial advisors can help ensure that your investment portfolio is aligned with your long-term financial goals and risk tolerance, while also considering tax-efficient strategies for estate planning purposes.

Conclusion:

As we conclude this chapter, I encourage you to consider the special considerations associated with managing complex assets in your estate plan, including real estate, businesses, and investments. By understanding the unique challenges and opportunities presented by these assets, you can develop a comprehensive plan that protects your legacy, minimizes tax liabilities, and provides for your loved ones effectively. In the chapters that follow, we'll continue to explore other critical aspects of the estate planning process and provide you with the knowledge and tools you need to create a plan that reflects your unique circumstances and priorities.

# Chapter 13: Utilizing Powers of Attorney and Advance Directives: Ensuring Decision-Making in Times of Incapacity

Welcome to Chapter 13 of "Will and Estate Planning." In this chapter, we'll explore the importance of utilizing powers of attorney and advance directives in your estate plan to ensure decision-making in times of incapacity. Planning for incapacity is a critical aspect of estate planning, as it allows you to appoint trusted individuals to make financial, medical, and personal decisions on your behalf if you become unable to do so yourself. By understanding the role of powers of attorney and advance directives, you can protect your interests and ensure that your wishes are followed even when you are unable to communicate them directly.

Powers of Attorney:

A power of attorney is a legal document that grants authority to another person (known as the agent or attorney-in-fact) to act on your behalf in financial and legal matters. In this section, we'll explore the different types of powers of attorney and their role in estate planning, including:

Financial Power of Attorney: This document authorizes your agent to manage your financial affairs, including paying bills, managing investments, and making financial decisions on your behalf. A durable power of attorney remains in effect even if you become incapacitated, providing continuity in managing your financial affairs.

Healthcare Power of Attorney: Also known as a medical power of attorney or healthcare proxy, this document allows your agent to make healthcare decisions on your behalf if you are unable to do so yourself. Your agent can communicate with healthcare providers, consent to, or refuse medical treatments, and make end-of-life decisions based on your wishes and values.

Advance Directives:

Advance directives are legal documents that allow you to express your healthcare preferences and end-of-life wishes in advance, ensuring that your wishes are followed even if you are unable to communicate them directly. In this section, we'll explore the different types of advance directives and their role in estate planning, including:

Living Will: A living will is a document that outlines your preferences for medical treatment and end-of-life care in the event that you are unable to communicate your wishes. It typically addresses issues such as life-sustaining treatment, resuscitation, and organ donation, providing guidance to healthcare providers and your loved ones.

Do-Not-Resuscitate (DNR) Order: A DNR order is a medical directive that instructs healthcare providers not to perform cardiopulmonary resuscitation (CPR) if your heart stops or if you stop breathing. It is typically used in situations where CPR would be futile or where you have expressed a desire to avoid aggressive medical interventions.

Physician Orders for Life-Sustaining Treatment (POLST): POLST forms are medical orders that translate your treatment preferences into actionable instructions for healthcare providers. They are typically used for individuals with serious or life-limiting illnesses and provide guidance on a range of medical interventions, including CPR, intubation, and artificial nutrition.

Considerations When Choosing Agents:

When appointing agents under powers of attorney and advance directives, it's essential to choose individuals who are trustworthy, competent, and capable of making decisions in your best interests. In this section, we'll discuss factors to consider when selecting agents, including:

Trustworthiness and Reliability: Your agents should be individuals whom you trust implicitly to act in your best interests and follow your wishes faithfully, even in difficult or stressful situations.

Competence and Qualifications: Your agents should have the knowledge, skills, and temperament necessary to make informed decisions on your behalf, particularly in complex or high-stakes situations.

Communication and Collaboration: Your agents should be willing and able to communicate effectively with healthcare providers, financial institutions, and other relevant parties, as well as collaborate with your other advisors, such as attorneys and financial planners.

Conclusion:

As we conclude this chapter, I encourage you to consider the importance of utilizing powers of attorney and advance directives in your estate plan to ensure decision-making in times of incapacity. By appointing trusted individuals to act on your behalf and expressing your healthcare preferences and end-of-life wishes in advance, you can protect your interests and ensure that your wishes are followed even when you are unable to communicate them directly. In the chapters that follow, we'll continue to explore other critical aspects of the estate planning process and provide you with the knowledge and tools you need to create a comprehensive plan that protects your assets and provides for your loved ones.

# Chapter 14: Charitable Giving Strategies: Leaving a Lasting Impact Through Philanthropy

Welcome to Chapter 14 of "Will and Estate Planning." In this chapter, we'll explore charitable giving strategies that enable you to leave a lasting impact through philanthropy. Charitable giving is a powerful way to support causes you care about, make a positive difference in the world, and leave a meaningful legacy for future generations. By understanding the various charitable giving strategies available, you can maximize the impact of your donations and ensure that your philanthropic goals are achieved in alignment with your overall estate plan.

Types of Charitable Giving:

Charitable giving can take many forms, each with its own benefits and considerations. In this section, we'll explore some common types of charitable giving, including:

Cash Donations: Direct cash donations are a simple and straightforward way to support charitable organizations. Cash gifts can be made outright or pledged over time, providing immediate support for charitable programs and initiatives. Appreciated Securities: Donating appreciated stocks, bonds, or mutual funds can offer significant tax benefits, including capital gains tax avoidance and potential income tax deductions for the fair market value of the donated assets.

Donor-Advised Funds (DAFs): DAFs are charitable giving vehicles that allow donors to make contributions to a fund managed by a sponsoring organization, such as a community foundation or financial institution. Donors can then recommend grants to qualified charitable organizations over time, providing flexibility and convenience in charitable giving.

Charitable Trusts: Charitable trusts, including charitable remainder trusts (CRTs) and charitable lead trusts (CLTs), offer advanced estate planning strategies that provide income to beneficiaries for a specified period before distributing the remaining assets to charitable organizations.

Bequests: Including charitable bequests in your will or trust allows you to leave a legacy for charitable causes while providing potential estate tax benefits for your heirs. Bequests can be made as specific dollar amounts, a percentage of your estate, or specific assets.

Benefits of Charitable Giving:

Charitable giving offers a range of benefits for donors, charitable organizations, and society as a whole. In this section, we'll explore some of the key benefits of charitable giving, including:

Tax Advantages: Charitable donations may be eligible for income tax deductions, capital gains tax avoidance, and estate tax benefits, providing potential tax savings for donors.

Fulfillment and Meaning: Charitable giving allows donors to support causes they are passionate about and make a meaningful difference in the lives of others, contributing to a sense of fulfillment and purpose.

Legacy and Impact: Charitable giving enables donors to leave a lasting legacy for future generations and create positive change in their communities and beyond, ensuring that their values and priorities endure.

Social Responsibility: Charitable giving demonstrates a commitment to social responsibility and philanthropy, helping to address pressing societal issues and promote positive social change.

Considerations for Effective Charitable Giving:

While charitable giving offers numerous benefits, it's essential to consider certain factors and best practices to maximize the impact of your donations. In this section, we'll discuss considerations for effective charitable giving, including:

Strategic Planning: Developing a charitable giving plan that aligns with your values, interests, and financial goals can help ensure that your donations have the greatest impact and support causes you care about deeply.

Due Diligence: Conducting research on charitable organizations to evaluate their mission, programs, financial health, and impact can help ensure that your donations are used effectively and efficiently to achieve meaningful outcomes.

Long-Term Engagement: Building relationships with charitable organizations and staying informed about their work allows donors to make informed decisions, provide ongoing support, and collaborate on shared goals over time.

Professional Guidance: Working with experienced advisors, such as financial planners, attorneys, and philanthropic consultants, can help donors navigate complex charitable giving strategies, maximize tax benefits, and achieve their philanthropic objectives.

Conclusion:

As we conclude this chapter, I encourage you to explore charitable giving strategies and consider how you can leave a lasting impact through philanthropy. Whether through cash donations, appreciated securities, charitable trusts, or other giving vehicles, charitable giving offers a powerful way to support causes you care about, make a positive difference in the world, and leave a meaningful legacy for future generations. In the chapters that follow, we'll continue to explore other critical aspects of the estate planning process and provide you with the knowledge and tools you need to create a comprehensive plan that reflects your values, priorities, and philanthropic aspirations.

# Chapter 15: Strategies for Minimizing Taxes and Maximizing Benefits

Welcome to Chapter 15 of "Will and Estate Planning." In this chapter, we'll explore strategies for minimizing taxes and maximizing benefits in your estate plan. Taxes can significantly impact the value of your estate and the distribution of your assets to your beneficiaries. By implementing tax-efficient strategies and taking advantage of available benefits, you can preserve more of your wealth for future generations and achieve your long-term financial goals.

Estate Tax Planning:

Estate taxes, also known as inheritance taxes or death taxes, are levied on the transfer of assets from a deceased individual to their heirs. In this section, we'll explore strategies for minimizing estate taxes, including:

Leveraging the Estate Tax Exemption: The estate tax exemption allows individuals to transfer a certain amount of assets tax-free to their heirs. By maximizing the use of the exemption through careful planning, such as gifting assets during your lifetime or using trusts, you can reduce the overall tax burden on your estate.

Spousal Portability: The concept of spousal portability allows a surviving spouse to inherit any unused portion of their deceased spouse's estate tax exemption, effectively doubling the amount that can be passed on to heirs tax-free. Proper planning to take advantage of spousal portability can result in significant tax savings for married couples.

Irrevocable Life Insurance Trusts (ILITs): ILITs are specialized trusts that hold life insurance policies outside of the insured's estate, allowing the death benefit to pass to beneficiaries free of estate taxes. Funding an ILIT with life insurance proceeds can provide liquidity to pay estate taxes and preserve other assets for your heirs.

Charitable Giving: Charitable bequests and donations can provide valuable estate tax deductions, reducing the taxable value of your estate and minimizing estate taxes. By including charitable gifts in your estate plan, you can support causes you care about while also benefiting from tax savings.

Income Tax Planning:

In addition to estate taxes, income taxes can also impact your estate and the distribution of your assets. In this section, we'll explore strategies for minimizing income taxes, including:

Basis Step-Up at Death: When assets are transferred at death, the recipient's cost basis is "stepped up" to the fair market value as of the date of death, eliminating any unrealized capital gains. Taking advantage of the basis step-up can reduce capital gains taxes for your heirs when they sell inherited assets.

Roth IRA Conversions: Converting traditional IRA assets to a Roth IRA can provide tax-free distributions for you and your heirs in the future. While Roth conversions involve paying taxes upfront, they can result in significant tax savings over time, particularly if you expect tax rates to increase in the future.

Qualified Charitable Distributions (QCDs): QCDs allow individuals aged 70½ or older to donate up to $100,000 annually from their IRA directly to charity, bypassing income taxes on the distribution. Making QCDs can satisfy required minimum distributions (RMDs) while also supporting charitable causes and reducing taxable income.

Gift Tax Planning:

Gift taxes apply to transfers of money or property during your lifetime, in addition to estate taxes. In this section, we'll explore strategies for minimizing gift taxes, including:

Annual Exclusion Gifts: Taking advantage of the annual gift tax exclusion allows you to make tax-free gifts of up to a certain amount ($15,000 per recipient in 2022) each year to an unlimited number of recipients. By making annual exclusion gifts, you can transfer assets to your heirs gradually over time without incurring gift taxes or using your lifetime gift tax exemption.

Lifetime Gift Tax Exemption: The lifetime gift tax exemption allows individuals to transfer a certain amount of assets tax-free over their lifetime ($12.06 million in 2022). By strategically gifting assets that are expected to appreciate in value, you can remove future appreciation from your estate and minimize estate taxes for your heirs.

Qualified Tuition and Medical Expenses: Payments made directly to educational institutions or medical providers for tuition or medical expenses on behalf of others are not considered taxable gifts, regardless of the amount. Taking advantage of these exclusions can provide tax-free support for education and healthcare costs for your loved ones.

Conclusion:

As we conclude this chapter, I encourage you to explore strategies for minimizing taxes and maximizing benefits in your estate plan. By implementing tax-efficient strategies tailored to your individual circumstances and objectives, you can preserve more of your wealth for future generations and achieve your long-term financial goals. In the chapters that follow, we'll continue to explore other critical aspects of the estate planning process and provide you with the knowledge and tools you need to create a comprehensive plan that protects your assets and provides for your loved ones.

# Chapter 16: Navigating Estate Taxes: Understanding Your Obligations and Opportunities

Welcome to Chapter 16 of "Will and Estate Planning." In this chapter, we'll navigate the complex landscape of estate taxes, helping you understand your obligations and opportunities when it comes to managing the tax implications of your estate. Estate taxes can significantly impact the distribution of your assets and the financial well-being of your heirs. By gaining a clear understanding of estate tax laws, exemptions, and planning strategies, you can minimize tax liabilities and preserve more of your wealth for future generations.

Understanding Estate Taxes:

Estate taxes, also known as inheritance taxes or death taxes, are levied on the transfer of assets from a deceased individual to their heirs. In this section, we'll explore the basics of estate taxes, including:

Estate Tax Thresholds: Estate tax laws establish thresholds that determine whether an estate is subject to taxation. For example, the federal estate tax applies to estates with a total taxable value exceeding $12.06 million in 2022, while some states have their own estate tax thresholds.

Tax Rates: Estate tax rates vary depending on the value of the taxable estate, with higher rates applied to larger estates. The federal estate tax rate ranges from 18% to 40% for taxable estates exceeding the exemption amount.

Exemptions and Deductions: Estate tax laws provide various exemptions and deductions that can reduce the taxable value of an estate, such as the unified credit against the federal estate tax and deductions for charitable bequests and estate administration expenses.

Strategies for Minimizing Estate Taxes:

Minimizing estate taxes requires careful planning and strategic implementation of tax-efficient strategies. In this section, we'll explore some common strategies for minimizing estate taxes, including:

Lifetime Gifting: Making gifts of assets during your lifetime can reduce the taxable value of your estate and take advantage of the annual gift tax exclusion and lifetime gift tax exemption.

Trust Planning: Establishing trusts, such as irrevocable life insurance trusts (ILITs), charitable remainder trusts (CRTs), and qualified personal residence trusts (QPRTs), can remove assets from your taxable estate while providing benefits for your beneficiaries and charitable causes.

Spousal Portability: Maximizing the use of spousal portability allows married couples to effectively double their combined estate tax exemptions, reducing or eliminating estate taxes for larger estates.

Charitable Giving: Including charitable bequests and donations in your estate plan can provide valuable estate tax deductions, reducing the taxable value of your estate while supporting causes you care about deeply.

State-Specific Considerations:

In addition to federal estate taxes, some states impose their own estate or inheritance taxes with different exemption amounts, rates, and rules. In this section, we'll explore state-specific considerations for estate tax planning, including:

State Estate Tax Thresholds: Understanding the estate tax thresholds and rates in your state can help you determine whether your estate may be subject to state estate taxes and plan accordingly.
State Estate Tax Exemptions and Deductions: Some states offer exemptions, deductions, or credits that can reduce state estate tax liabilities, such as deductions for bequests to spouses or charitable organizations.
Professional Guidance and Compliance:

Navigating estate taxes requires careful consideration of complex laws and regulations. In this section, we'll discuss the importance of seeking professional guidance from experienced estate planning attorneys, tax advisors, and financial planners to ensure compliance with estate tax laws and optimize tax-efficient strategies for your individual circumstances.

Conclusion:

As we conclude this chapter, I encourage you to take proactive steps to navigate estate taxes effectively and minimize tax liabilities in your estate plan. By understanding your obligations and opportunities regarding estate taxes, seeking professional guidance, and implementing tax-efficient strategies tailored to your individual circumstances, you can preserve more of your wealth for future generations and achieve your long-term financial goals. In the chapters that follow, we'll continue to explore other critical aspects of the estate planning process and provide you with the knowledge and tools you need to create a comprehensive plan that protects your assets and provides for your loved ones.

# Chapter 17: Leveraging Tax-Advantaged Accounts: IRAs, 401(k)s, and Other Retirement Vehicles

Welcome to Chapter 17 of "Will and Estate Planning." In this chapter, we'll explore the strategic use of tax-advantaged retirement accounts, such as Individual Retirement Accounts (IRAs), 401(k)s, and other retirement vehicles, in your estate plan. These accounts offer valuable tax benefits during your lifetime and can play a significant role in preserving and transferring wealth to your beneficiaries. By understanding the rules, opportunities, and considerations associated with tax-advantaged retirement accounts, you can optimize their use as part of your overall estate planning strategy.

Understanding Tax-Advantaged Retirement Accounts:

Tax-advantaged retirement accounts are investment vehicles designed to help individuals save for retirement while enjoying certain tax benefits. In this section, we'll explore some common types of tax-advantaged retirement accounts, including:

Traditional IRAs: Traditional IRAs allow individuals to make tax-deductible contributions, defer taxes on investment earnings until withdrawals are made in retirement, and potentially lower their taxable income during their working years.
Roth IRAs: Roth IRAs offer tax-free growth and withdrawals for qualified distributions, allowing individuals to contribute after-tax dollars and enjoy tax-free retirement income in the future.
Employer-Sponsored Retirement Plans: Employer-sponsored retirement plans, such as 401(k)s, 403(b)s, and 457(b) plans, offer tax-deferred growth, employer matching contributions, and higher contribution limits compared to IRAs.

Self-Employed Retirement Plans: Self-employed individuals and small business owners may have access to specialized retirement plans, such as Simplified Employee Pension (SEP) IRAs and Solo 401(k)s, which offer higher contribution limits and tax benefits for business owners.

Strategies for Maximizing Tax Benefits:

Maximizing the tax benefits of retirement accounts requires careful planning and strategic implementation of tax-efficient strategies. In this section, we'll explore some common strategies for leveraging tax-advantaged retirement accounts in your estate plan, including:

Traditional IRA Conversions: Converting traditional IRA assets to a Roth IRA can provide tax-free growth and withdrawals in retirement, potentially reducing future tax liabilities for you and your heirs.

Stretch IRA Planning: Naming younger beneficiaries, such as children or grandchildren, as beneficiaries of your retirement accounts can enable them to "stretch" distributions over their life expectancy, maximizing tax-deferred growth and minimizing immediate tax obligations.

Charitable Giving Strategies: Using retirement assets to fund charitable bequests or donations can provide valuable estate tax deductions and avoid income taxes for your heirs, making retirement accounts an efficient vehicle for charitable giving.

Estate Planning Trusts: Establishing trusts as beneficiaries of your retirement accounts can provide asset protection, control, and flexibility in distributing retirement assets to your heirs while potentially minimizing income and estate taxes.

Considerations and Compliance:

When incorporating tax-advantaged retirement accounts into your estate plan, it's essential to consider various factors and comply with applicable rules and regulations. In this section, we'll discuss considerations for managing retirement accounts in your estate plan, including:

Required Minimum Distributions (RMDs): Understanding RMD rules and deadlines is crucial to avoid penalties and ensure compliance with IRS regulations for distributions from tax-deferred retirement accounts.
Beneficiary Designations: Carefully selecting beneficiaries and updating beneficiary designations regularly can help ensure that your retirement assets are distributed according to your wishes and aligned with your estate planning objectives.
Tax Implications: Recognizing the tax implications of different distribution strategies, such as lump-sum distributions, periodic withdrawals, or annuitization, can help you make informed decisions about managing retirement account distributions in retirement and beyond.
Conclusion:

As we conclude this chapter, I encourage you to explore the strategic use of tax-advantaged retirement accounts in your estate plan. By understanding the rules, opportunities, and considerations associated with IRAs, 401(k)s, and other retirement vehicles, you can maximize tax benefits, preserve more of your wealth for future generations, and achieve your long-term financial goals. In the chapters that follow, we'll continue to explore other critical aspects of the estate planning process and provide you with the knowledge and tools you need to create a comprehensive plan that protects your assets and provides for your loved ones.

# Chapter 18: Maximizing Social Security and Pension Benefits: Planning for Retirement Income Streams

Welcome to Chapter 18 of "Will and Estate Planning." In this chapter, we'll delve into the strategies for maximizing Social Security and pension benefits as essential components of your retirement income streams. Social Security and pension benefits provide a crucial source of financial support during retirement, and understanding how to optimize these benefits can significantly impact your financial security in your golden years. By exploring the rules, options, and considerations associated with Social Security and pension benefits, you can make informed decisions to enhance your retirement income and achieve your long-term financial goals.

Maximizing Social Security Benefits:

Social Security benefits are a foundation of retirement income for millions of Americans. In this section, we'll explore strategies for maximizing Social Security benefits, including:

Delayed Retirement Credits: Delaying claiming Social Security benefits beyond your full retirement age (FRA) can increase your monthly benefit amount through delayed retirement credits, up to age 70.
Spousal and Survivor Benefits: Spouses may be eligible to claim spousal benefits based on their partner's work record, while surviving spouses may be entitled to survivor benefits. Coordinating spousal and survivor benefits can maximize household income over the long term.
File and Suspend Strategies: File and suspend strategies allow one spouse to claim benefits at full retirement age while the other spouse delays claiming to accrue delayed retirement credits, maximizing household benefits.
Coordination with Other Retirement Income: Integrating Social Security benefits with other retirement income sources, such as pensions, IRAs, and annuities, can optimize cash flow and tax efficiency during retirement.
Maximizing Pension Benefits:

Pension benefits provide a reliable stream of income for retirees with employer-sponsored retirement plans. In this section, we'll explore strategies for maximizing pension benefits, including:

Understanding Plan Options: Understanding the various payout options available through your pension plan, such as single-life annuities, joint-and-survivor annuities, and lump-sum distributions, can help you choose the option that best meets your financial needs and retirement goals.

Pension Maximization Strategies: Pension maximization strategies involve selecting the highest-paying pension option available and using life insurance to provide survivor benefits for your spouse or beneficiaries. This approach can maximize pension income while preserving flexibility and control over retirement assets.

Coordination with Social Security: Coordinating pension benefits with Social Security benefits and other retirement income sources can help you optimize overall retirement income and manage tax liabilities effectively.

Considerations and Decision-Making:

When planning for Social Security and pension benefits, it's essential to consider various factors and make informed decisions based on your individual circumstances and objectives. In this section, we'll discuss considerations and decision-making strategies for maximizing retirement income streams, including:

Longevity and Health Considerations: Considering factors such as life expectancy, health status, and anticipated healthcare costs can help you determine the optimal timing and claiming strategy for Social Security and pension benefits.

Financial Planning and Tax Optimization: Integrating Social Security and pension benefits into your overall financial plan, including tax planning strategies and investment considerations, can help you maximize retirement income and minimize tax liabilities over the long term.

Professional Guidance: Seeking guidance from financial advisors, retirement planners, and estate planning professionals can provide valuable insights and expertise to navigate complex retirement income decisions and optimize benefits effectively.

Conclusion:

As we conclude this chapter, I encourage you to explore the strategies for maximizing Social Security and pension benefits as essential components of your retirement income streams. By understanding the rules, options, and considerations associated with Social Security and pension benefits, you can make informed decisions to enhance your retirement income, achieve financial security, and enjoy a fulfilling retirement. In the chapters that follow, we'll continue to explore other critical aspects of the estate planning process and provide you with the knowledge and tools you need to create a comprehensive plan that protects your assets and provides for your loved ones.

# Chapter 19: Addressing Family Dynamics and Potential Challenges

Welcome to Chapter 19 of "Will and Estate Planning." In this chapter, we'll address the importance of understanding family dynamics and potential challenges in the estate planning process. Family dynamics can play a significant role in shaping estate planning decisions and outcomes, and addressing potential challenges proactively can help preserve family harmony, minimize conflicts, and ensure that your wishes are carried out effectively. By exploring common family dynamics and potential challenges in estate planning, you can develop strategies to navigate sensitive issues and create a comprehensive plan that reflects your values, priorities, and goals for your legacy.

Understanding Family Dynamics:

Every family is unique, with its own dynamics, relationships, and communication styles. In this section, we'll explore some common family dynamics that may impact the estate planning process, including:

Family Structure: Blended families, multi-generational households, and non-traditional family structures can present unique challenges and considerations in estate planning, such as competing interests among family members and complex distribution preferences.
Communication Patterns: Open and honest communication among family members is essential for effective estate planning. Communication barriers, conflicts, and unresolved issues can hinder the planning process and lead to misunderstandings or disputes down the line.
Interpersonal Relationships: Strong family relationships, trust, and mutual respect are critical for successful estate planning. Strained relationships, resentments, or unresolved conflicts among family members can complicate decision-making and create tensions during the planning process.

Cultural and Value Differences: Cultural backgrounds, values, and beliefs can influence estate planning preferences and priorities, such as attitudes towards inheritance, philanthropy, and family obligations.

Addressing Potential Challenges:

Anticipating and addressing potential challenges in the estate planning process is essential for preserving family harmony and ensuring that your wishes are carried out effectively. In this section, we'll explore some common challenges and strategies for addressing them, including:

Lack of Communication: Encouraging open and honest communication among family members about estate planning goals, intentions, and expectations can foster understanding, reduce misunderstandings, and build consensus around key decisions.

Unequal Inheritances: Discussing unequal inheritances openly and transparently with family members can help manage expectations, mitigate potential conflicts, and provide clarity about the reasoning behind distribution decisions.

Family Conflicts and Disputes: Implementing conflict resolution strategies, such as mediation or family meetings facilitated by a neutral third party, can help resolve disagreements, bridge differences, and foster collaboration among family members.

Contesting the Will: Taking proactive steps to minimize the risk of will contests, such as ensuring the validity of legal documents, providing clear explanations for distribution decisions, and maintaining thorough records of the planning process, can help prevent disputes and uphold the integrity of your estate plan.

Promoting Family Unity and Collaboration:

Promoting family unity and collaboration is essential for successful estate planning and legacy preservation. In this section, we'll explore strategies for promoting family unity and collaboration in the estate planning process, including:

Involving Family Members: Involving family members in the estate planning process and soliciting their input, feedback, and perspectives can foster a sense of ownership, engagement, and shared responsibility for the family's legacy.
Educating and Empowering Heirs: Providing education and guidance to heirs about estate planning principles, responsibilities, and expectations can empower them to participate actively in the planning process and prepare for their roles as stewards of the family legacy.
Emphasizing Shared Values: Emphasizing shared values, goals, and aspirations can unify family members around a common vision for the family's legacy and promote collaboration in achieving collective objectives.
Cultivating Trust and Transparency: Cultivating trust, transparency, and accountability in family relationships and estate planning decisions can strengthen family bonds, promote open communication, and mitigate conflicts or misunderstandings.
Conclusion:

As we conclude this chapter, I encourage you to consider the importance of addressing family dynamics and potential challenges in the estate planning process. By understanding family dynamics, anticipating potential challenges, and implementing strategies to promote family unity and collaboration, you can navigate sensitive issues, preserve family harmony, and ensure that your estate plan reflects your values, priorities, and goals for your legacy. In the chapters that follow, we'll continue to explore other critical aspects of the estate planning process and provide you with the knowledge and tools you need to create a comprehensive plan that protects your assets and provides for your loved ones.

# Chapter 20: Communicating Your Intentions: Discussing Your Estate Plan With Loved Ones

Welcome to Chapter 20 of "Will and Estate Planning." In this chapter, we'll explore the importance of communicating your intentions and discussing your estate plan with your loved ones. Effective communication about your estate plan can foster understanding, transparency, and trust among family members, minimize misunderstandings or conflicts, and ensure that your wishes are carried out according to your intentions. By engaging in open and honest conversations about your estate plan, you can empower your loved ones to support your decisions and prepare for their roles in the implementation of your legacy.

The Importance of Communication:

Effective communication is essential for successful estate planning and legacy preservation. In this section, we'll explore why communication about your estate plan is important, including:

Clarifying Intentions: Communicating your intentions and objectives for your estate plan helps ensure that your wishes are understood and followed by your loved ones and beneficiaries.

Building Trust: Open and honest communication fosters trust and transparency among family members, empowering them to support your decisions and work together collaboratively.

Managing Expectations: Discussing your estate plan with your loved ones helps manage expectations about inheritances, distribution decisions, and responsibilities, reducing the risk of misunderstandings or conflicts in the future.

Empowering Heirs: Engaging in conversations about your estate plan empowers your heirs to understand their roles, responsibilities, and expectations, preparing them to fulfill their duties as stewards of your legacy.

Guidelines for Effective Communication:

Communicating your intentions and discussing your estate plan with your loved ones requires careful consideration and planning. In this section, we'll explore some guidelines for effective communication about your estate plan, including:

Choose the Right Time and Setting: Selecting an appropriate time and setting for discussing your estate plan, such as during a family meeting or a private conversation, can create a comfortable and conducive environment for open dialogue.

Be Clear and Direct: Clearly and directly communicate your intentions, wishes, and expectations for your estate plan, using straightforward language and providing context or explanations as needed.

Listen and Validate: Actively listen to the perspectives, concerns, and questions of your loved ones, validating their feelings and experiences and addressing any uncertainties or misunderstandings with empathy and patience.

Respect Privacy and Boundaries: Respect the privacy and boundaries of your loved ones when discussing sensitive topics related to your estate plan, recognizing their autonomy and individual perspectives.

Offer Support and Resources: Offer support and resources to your loved ones as they navigate the estate planning process, providing guidance, information, and access to professional advisors or resources as needed.

Addressing Sensitive Topics:

Discussing your estate plan may involve addressing sensitive topics or emotions. In this section, we'll explore strategies for addressing sensitive topics with sensitivity and empathy, including:

Family Relationships: Acknowledge the importance of family relationships and dynamics in estate planning discussions, demonstrating sensitivity to individual feelings and perspectives.

Inheritance and Fairness: Address concerns about inheritance and fairness openly and honestly, explaining distribution decisions and considering alternative perspectives with empathy and understanding.

End-of-Life Wishes: Discuss end-of-life wishes and healthcare directives with compassion and sensitivity, emphasizing the importance of honoring individual preferences and values.

Conclusion:

As we conclude this chapter, I encourage you to consider the importance of communicating your intentions and discussing your estate plan with your loved ones. By engaging in open and honest conversations about your estate plan, you can foster understanding, trust, and collaboration among family members, minimize misunderstandings or conflicts, and ensure that your wishes are carried out according to your intentions. In the chapters that follow, we'll continue to explore other critical aspects of the estate planning process and provide you with the knowledge and tools you need to create a comprehensive plan that protects your assets and provides for your loved ones.

# Chapter 21: Handling Blended Families and Complex Relationships: Strategies for Fair and Equitable Distribution

Welcome to Chapter 21 of "Will and Estate Planning." In this chapter, we'll explore strategies for handling blended families and complex relationships in estate planning to ensure fair and equitable distribution of assets. Blended families, comprising individuals with children from previous relationships, present unique challenges, and considerations when it comes to estate planning. By understanding the dynamics of blended families and implementing strategies to address complex relationships sensitively and effectively, you can protect your legacy, minimize conflicts, and ensure that your loved ones are provided for according to your wishes.

Understanding Blended Families and Complex Relationships:

Blended families encompass diverse family structures and relationships, including second marriages, stepchildren, half-siblings, and extended family members. In this section, we'll explore some common characteristics of blended families and complex relationships in estate planning, including:

Multiple Spouses and Partners: Blended families may involve individuals who have been married or in committed relationships multiple times, leading to complex dynamics and competing interests among spouses or partners.
Stepchildren and Half-Siblings: Blended families often include stepchildren and half-siblings with different biological or legal relationships to each other and to the deceased individual, raising questions about inheritance rights and fair treatment.
Unequal Contributions and Responsibilities: Blended families may involve individuals with unequal financial contributions, responsibilities, and caregiving roles within the family, complicating distribution decisions and potential conflicts over inheritance.
Strategies for Fair and Equitable Distribution:

Navigating estate planning for blended families requires careful consideration and strategic planning to ensure fair and equitable distribution of assets. In this section, we'll explore some strategies for handling blended families and complex relationships sensitively and effectively, including:

Open Communication: Foster open and honest communication among family members about estate planning goals, intentions, and expectations, encouraging transparency, understanding, and collaboration.
Customized Estate Planning Solutions: Tailor your estate plan to address the unique needs and circumstances of your blended family, considering factors such as prenuptial agreements, marital property laws, and distribution preferences.
Use of Trusts: Establish trusts as part of your estate plan to provide for specific beneficiaries, such as children from previous relationships, while protecting assets, maintaining control, and minimizing potential conflicts.

Fairness vs. Equality: Consider the distinction between fairness and equality in estate planning for blended families, recognizing that fair distribution may not always mean equal distribution and adjusting inheritance provisions accordingly.
Preparing for Contingencies: Anticipate potential contingencies and life events, such as remarriage, divorce, or changes in family dynamics, when drafting your estate plan, and regularly review and update your plan as needed to reflect changing circumstances.
Addressing Emotional Considerations:

In addition to legal and financial considerations, estate planning for blended families often involves navigating emotional complexities and sensitivities. In this section, we'll explore strategies for addressing emotional considerations in estate planning, including:

Respect and Empathy: Approach estate planning discussions with respect, empathy, and sensitivity to individual feelings and perspectives, recognizing the emotional significance of inheritance and family relationships.
Family Meetings and Mediation: Facilitate family meetings or mediation sessions with the assistance of a neutral third party to address concerns, resolve conflicts, and foster understanding and consensus among family members.
Legacy Planning and Shared Values: Emphasize legacy planning and shared values as guiding principles in estate planning for blended families, encouraging family members to focus on common goals and aspirations for the family's legacy.
Conclusion:

As we conclude this chapter, I encourage you to consider the strategies for handling blended families and complex relationships in estate planning to ensure fair and equitable distribution of assets. By understanding the dynamics of blended families, implementing customized estate planning solutions, and addressing emotional considerations sensitively and effectively, you can protect your legacy, minimize conflicts, and ensure that your loved ones are provided for according to your wishes. In the chapters that follow, we'll continue to explore other critical aspects of the estate planning process and provide you with the knowledge and tools you need to create a comprehensive plan that protects your assets and provides for your loved ones.

# Chapter 22: Planning for Incapacity and End-of-Life Care: Health Care Directives and Medical Decision-Making

Welcome to Chapter 22 of "Will and Estate Planning." In this chapter, we'll explore the importance of planning for incapacity and end-of-life care through the use of health care directives and medical decision-making strategies. Planning for incapacity involves making arrangements for medical care and decision-making in the event that you become unable to make decisions for yourself due to illness, injury, or cognitive decline. By proactively addressing these issues and documenting your preferences for medical treatment and end-of-life care, you can ensure that your wishes are respected and that you receive the care you desire during times of incapacity.

Understanding Health Care Directives:

Health care directives, also known as advance directives or living wills, are legal documents that allow you to specify your preferences for medical treatment and end-of-life care in advance. In this section, we'll explore the purpose and components of health care directives, including:

Medical Treatment Preferences: Health care directives allow you to specify the types of medical treatments you wish to receive or refuse in the event that you are unable to communicate your wishes, such as life-sustaining treatments, resuscitation efforts, or pain management.

End-of-Life Care Preferences: Health care directives enable you to express your preferences for end-of-life care, such as whether you wish to receive palliative care, hospice care, or comfort measures in the final stages of life.

Appointment of Health Care Proxy: Health care directives often include provisions for appointing a health care proxy or agent to make medical decisions on your behalf if you are unable to do so yourself, ensuring that your wishes are honored and communicated effectively.

Navigating Medical Decision-Making:

Navigating medical decision-making involves understanding the legal and ethical principles governing health care decisions and ensuring that your wishes are followed in accordance with applicable laws and regulations. In this section, we'll explore some key considerations for navigating medical decision-making, including:

Legal Requirements: Familiarize yourself with the legal requirements for health care directives and medical decision-making in your state or jurisdiction, including rules for executing and witnessing advance directives and the authority of health care proxies.

Communication with Health Care Providers: Communicate your preferences for medical treatment and end-of-life care with your health care providers, ensuring that they are aware of your wishes and can help facilitate appropriate care during times of incapacity.

Review and Update: Regularly review and update your health care directives to reflect changes in your health status, treatment preferences, or personal circumstances, ensuring that your wishes remain current and accurately documented.
Family and Caregiver Communication: Discuss your health care directives and medical preferences with your family members, caregivers, and other relevant individuals, ensuring that they understand your wishes and are prepared to advocate on your behalf if necessary.
Preparing for End-of-Life Care:

Preparing for end-of-life care involves considering your preferences for comfort, dignity, and quality of life in the final stages of life and making arrangements to ensure that your wishes are respected and honored. In this section, we'll explore some considerations for preparing for end-of-life care, including:

Palliative Care and Hospice Services: Consider your preferences for palliative care and hospice services, which focus on relieving pain and improving quality of life for individuals with serious illnesses or conditions, and discuss these preferences with your health care providers and loved ones.
Funeral and Burial Planning: Consider your preferences for funeral arrangements, burial or cremation, and memorial services, and document these preferences in advance to ensure that your wishes are carried out and relieve the burden on your loved ones during a difficult time.
Emotional and Spiritual Support: Seek emotional and spiritual support from your loved ones, clergy, or other sources of comfort and guidance, recognizing the importance of holistic care and support during the end-of-life journey.
Conclusion:

As we conclude this chapter, I encourage you to consider the importance of planning for incapacity and end-of-life care through the use of health care directives and medical decision-making strategies. By documenting your preferences for medical treatment and end-of-life care in advance, communicating these preferences with your loved ones and health care providers, and preparing for the emotional and practical aspects of end-of-life care.

# Chapter 23: Putting Your Plan Into Action

Welcome to Chapter 23 of "Will and Estate Planning." In this chapter, we'll explore the practical steps involved in putting your estate plan into action. After carefully crafting your estate plan and documenting your wishes, it's essential to take proactive steps to implement your plan effectively, ensuring that your intentions are carried out according to your wishes and that your loved ones are prepared to execute your plan when the time comes.

Executing Your Estate Plan:

Executing your estate plan involves taking the necessary legal and administrative steps to formalize your plan and ensure its validity and enforceability. In this section, we'll explore some key steps involved in executing your estate plan, including:

Reviewing Legal Documents: Review your will, trust documents, health care directives, powers of attorney, and other legal documents carefully to ensure that they accurately reflect your wishes and are executed in accordance with applicable laws and regulations.
Signing and Witnessing: Sign your legal documents in the presence of witnesses and a notary public as required by law to ensure their validity and enforceability, following the proper procedures and formalities for execution.

Distributing Copies: Distribute copies of your legal documents to your appointed executors, trustees, agents, and other relevant individuals, ensuring that they have access to the information and instructions they need to carry out your wishes effectively.

Communicating Your Plan: Communicate your estate plan and wishes with your loved ones, beneficiaries, and other relevant individuals, providing explanations, guidance, and reassurance as needed to ensure understanding and support.

Organizing Your Affairs:

Organizing your affairs involves gathering and organizing important documents, information, and records related to your estate plan and financial affairs. In this section, we'll explore some strategies for organizing your affairs effectively, including:

Creating a Document Inventory: Compile a comprehensive inventory of your legal documents, financial accounts, insurance policies, real estate holdings, digital assets, and other assets and liabilities, organizing them in a secure and accessible format for easy reference.

Establishing a Filing System: Establish a filing system or digital repository to store and organize your important documents and records, using folders, labels, and categories to facilitate retrieval and organization.

Designating Key Contacts: Designate key contacts, such as your executor, trustee, attorney, financial advisor, and insurance agent, and provide them with access to your document inventory and filing system to facilitate communication and coordination.

Updating Regularly: Regularly review and update your document inventory and filing system to reflect changes in your circumstances, financial status, or estate planning objectives, ensuring that your information remains current and accurate over time.

Preparing Your Executors and Trustees:

Preparing your executors and trustees involves ensuring that the individuals appointed to manage your estate and trust affairs are informed, capable, and prepared to fulfill their duties effectively. In this section, we'll explore some strategies for preparing your executors and trustees, including:

Providing Instructions: Provide clear and detailed instructions to your executors and trustees regarding their roles, responsibilities, and duties under your estate plan, explaining your intentions, expectations, and preferences for asset management and distribution.

Educating and Training: Educate your executors and trustees about the legal and financial aspects of estate and trust administration, providing resources, training, and guidance to help them understand their obligations and navigate the process effectively.

Facilitating Access: Facilitate access to relevant information, documents, and resources for your executors and trustees, ensuring that they have the support and assistance they need to carry out their duties efficiently and responsibly.

Conclusion:

As we conclude this chapter and our comprehensive guide to estate planning, I encourage you to take the necessary steps to put your estate plan into action effectively. By executing your legal documents, organizing your affairs, and preparing your executors and trustees, you can ensure that your wishes are carried out according to your intentions and that your loved ones are equipped to manage your affairs responsibly and effectively. Remember that estate planning is an ongoing process, and it's essential to review and update your plan regularly to reflect changes in your circumstances, financial status, or estate planning objectives. With careful planning and proactive action, you can protect your assets, provide for your loved ones, and secure your legacy for generations to come.

# Chapter 24: Working With Legal Professionals: Finding the Right Estate Planning Attorney

Welcome to Chapter 24 of "Will and Estate Planning." In this chapter, we'll discuss the importance of working with legal professionals, particularly estate planning attorneys, to ensure that your estate plan is comprehensive, legally sound, and tailored to your specific needs and objectives. Finding the right estate planning attorney is crucial for navigating the complexities of estate planning and drafting legal documents that accurately reflect your wishes and intentions. By partnering with a knowledgeable and experienced attorney, you can gain peace of mind knowing that your estate plan is in capable hands and that your legacy will be protected according to your wishes.

The Role of Estate Planning Attorneys:

Estate planning attorneys specialize in helping individuals and families create comprehensive estate plans that address their unique needs, goals, and circumstances. In this section, we'll explore the role of estate planning attorneys and the services they provide, including:

Legal Expertise: Estate planning attorneys possess specialized knowledge of estate planning laws, regulations, and strategies, allowing them to provide informed guidance and advice tailored to your individual situation.
Customized Solutions: Estate planning attorneys work closely with clients to understand their objectives, preferences, and concerns, developing customized solutions and drafting legal documents that reflect their wishes and intentions.
Document Preparation: Estate planning attorneys draft and prepare a variety of legal documents, including wills, trusts, powers of attorney, health care directives, and beneficiary designations, ensuring that they are properly executed and legally enforceable.
Review and Updates: Estate planning attorneys review and update clients' estate plans regularly to reflect changes in their circumstances, financial status, or estate planning goals, ensuring that their plans remain current and effective over time.
Finding the Right Estate Planning Attorney:

Finding the right estate planning attorney is essential for creating a comprehensive and effective estate plan. In this section, we'll explore some tips and considerations for finding and selecting the right estate planning attorney for your needs, including:

Research and Referrals: Research estate planning attorneys in your area and seek referrals from trusted sources, such as friends, family members, financial advisors, or legal professionals, who have experience working with estate planning attorneys.

Experience and Specialization: Look for estate planning attorneys with experience and expertise in estate planning law, particularly in areas relevant to your situation, such as wills, trusts, tax planning, and asset protection.

Credentials and Reputation: Consider the credentials, qualifications, and reputation of estate planning attorneys, such as their education, professional memberships, awards, and client reviews, to assess their credibility and trustworthiness.

Consultations and Interviews: Schedule consultations or interviews with prospective estate planning attorneys to discuss your needs, objectives, and concerns, and evaluate their communication style, responsiveness, and compatibility with your personality and preferences.

Fee Structure and Costs: Clarify the fee structure and costs associated with estate planning services, including hourly rates, flat fees, or retainer agreements, and ensure that you understand the scope of services covered and any additional charges or expenses.

Conclusion:

As we conclude this chapter, I encourage you to recognize the importance of working with legal professionals, particularly estate planning attorneys, to create a comprehensive and effective estate plan. By partnering with an experienced and knowledgeable attorney, you can ensure that your wishes are accurately documented, legally enforceable, and tailored to your specific needs and objectives. Remember to research, interview, and select the right estate planning attorney for your needs, considering factors such as experience, specialization, credentials, reputation, and compatibility. With the guidance and expertise of a trusted estate planning attorney, you can navigate the complexities of estate planning with confidence and peace of mind, knowing that your legacy will be protected and your loved ones provided for according to your wishes.

## Chapter 25: Conclusion

Embracing Peace of Mind: The Power of a Well-Crafted Estate Plan

As we reach the conclusion of "Will and Estate Planning", it's essential to reflect on the significance of a well-crafted estate plan in providing peace of mind and security for you and your loved ones. Throughout this guide, we've explored the various elements of estate planning, from setting goals and understanding legal concepts to executing documents and preparing for the future. Now, let's take a moment to appreciate the power and impact of a thoughtfully designed estate plan.

Your estate plan is more than just a collection of legal documents; it's a reflection of your values, priorities, and aspirations for the future. By taking proactive steps to plan for your legacy, you're not only protecting your assets and providing for your loved ones but also ensuring that your wishes are honored and your values preserved for generations to come.

A well-crafted estate plan empowers you to:

Protect Your Assets: By establishing wills, trusts, and other legal instruments, you can protect your assets from unnecessary taxes, creditors, and other threats, preserving your hard-earned wealth for your beneficiaries.

Provide for Your Loved Ones: Your estate plan allows you to provide for your loved ones according to your wishes, ensuring that they are cared for financially and emotionally in the event of your incapacity or passing.

Preserve Family Harmony: By communicating your intentions, addressing potential conflicts, and promoting transparency and fairness in your estate plan, you can minimize disputes and preserve family harmony for future generations.

Plan for the Unexpected: Estate planning isn't just about preparing for the inevitable; it's also about planning for the unexpected. By addressing contingencies, such as incapacity or changes in circumstances, you can ensure that your affairs are handled according to your wishes, even in challenging situations.

Moving Forward With Confidence: Taking Control of Your Future and Securing Your Legacy

As you move forward with confidence, armed with the knowledge and tools provided in this guide, remember that estate planning is an ongoing process. Life is full of changes, and your estate plan should evolve with you to reflect new priorities, milestones, and challenges along the way.

Here are some key steps to continue taking control of your future and securing your legacy:

Regular Review and Updates: Review your estate plan regularly, at least every few years or whenever significant life events occur, such as marriage, divorce, birth, death, or changes in financial status.

Communication and Education: Keep your loved ones informed about your estate plan and encourage open communication about your wishes, intentions, and expectations for the future.

Professional Guidance: Consult with legal, financial, and tax professionals as needed to ensure that your estate plan remains current, compliant, and optimized for your unique circumstances.

Legacy Building: Consider how you can use your estate plan to leave a lasting impact on your community, society, or future generations through charitable giving, philanthropy, or other legacy-building initiatives.

By embracing peace of mind and taking proactive steps to secure your legacy, you're not only providing for your loved ones but also leaving a meaningful and lasting imprint on the world. Your estate plan is a testament to your values, your vision, and your enduring commitment to the well-being of those you cherish most. As you embark on this journey, may you find clarity, confidence, and fulfillment in knowing that your legacy is in capable hands, and your wishes will be honored for generations to come.

# Glossary of Estate Planning Terms and Conditions

Advance Directive: A legal document that allows individuals to specify their preferences for medical treatment and end-of-life care in the event of incapacity.

Beneficiary: An individual or entity designated to receive assets or benefits from a will, trust, insurance policy, retirement account, or other estate planning instrument.

Estate: The total value of a person's assets, including real estate, personal property, investments, and financial accounts, minus any debts or liabilities.

Estate Planning: The process of arranging for the management and distribution of an individual's assets and affairs during their lifetime and after their death, typically to achieve specific financial, personal, and philanthropic goals.

Executor: A person or entity appointed in a will to carry out the instructions and administer the estate of a deceased individual, including gathering assets, paying debts, and distributing property to beneficiaries.

Fiduciary: A person or entity legally entrusted with the responsibility to act in the best interests of another party, such as an executor, trustee, or agent under a power of attorney.

Guardian: A person appointed by a court to make legal and personal decisions on behalf of a minor child or incapacitated adult who is unable to make decisions for themselves.

Health Care Proxy: A legal document that appoints a trusted individual, known as a health care agent or proxy, to make medical decisions on behalf of an individual who is unable to do so themselves.

Intestate: The legal status of dying without a valid will or estate plan in place, resulting in the distribution of assets according to state laws of intestacy.

Living Trust: A legal arrangement in which a person (the grantor) transfers ownership of assets to a trust during their lifetime, with a designated trustee responsible for managing the assets and distributing them to beneficiaries according to the terms of the trust document.

Power of Attorney: A legal document that grants authority to another person (the agent or attorney-in-fact) to act on behalf of the principal in financial, legal, or medical matters.

Probate: The court-supervised process of validating a will, settling debts, and distributing assets of a deceased person's estate according to their will or state laws if there is no will.

Trust: A legal entity created to hold and manage assets on behalf of beneficiaries, typically established to achieve specific estate planning goals, such as asset protection, privacy, or tax efficiency.

Will: A legal document that outlines a person's wishes for the distribution of their assets and the appointment of guardians for minor children upon their death.

These definitions provide a foundation for understanding key terms and concepts related to estate planning. It's essential to consult with legal and financial professionals to tailor your estate plan to your unique needs and objectives.

# Estate Planning Checklist

Assess Your Assets and Liabilities:

Compile a list of all your assets, including real estate, investments, bank accounts, retirement accounts, life insurance policies, and personal property.
Determine your liabilities, including mortgages, loans, credit card debt, and other obligations.
Set Your Goals and Objectives:

Define your estate planning goals, such as providing for your loved ones, minimizing taxes, protecting assets, and ensuring your wishes are carried out.
Consider your long-term financial and personal objectives, including retirement planning, charitable giving, and legacy preservation.
Create or Update Your Will:

Draft a will that outlines your wishes for the distribution of your assets and the appointment of guardians for minor children.
Review and update your will regularly to reflect changes in your circumstances, family dynamics, or estate planning goals.
Establish Trusts, if Appropriate:

Consider establishing trusts to protect assets, provide for specific beneficiaries, and minimize estate taxes.

Determine the type of trust(s) that align with your goals, such as revocable living trusts, irrevocable trusts, or special needs trusts.

Designate Beneficiaries:

Review beneficiary designations on retirement accounts, life insurance policies, and other assets to ensure they reflect your current wishes.

Consider contingent beneficiaries in case your primary beneficiaries predecease you.

Prepare Advance Directives:

Create a durable power of attorney to appoint someone to make financial and legal decisions on your behalf if you become incapacitated.

Draft a healthcare proxy or medical power of attorney to designate a trusted individual to make medical decisions for you if you are unable to do so.

Consider End-of-Life Care:

Document your preferences for end-of-life care, including life-sustaining treatments, palliative care, and hospice services.

Communicate your wishes with your healthcare providers and loved ones to ensure they are aware of your preferences.

Review and Update Insurance Policies:

Review your life insurance policies, disability insurance, and long-term care insurance coverage to ensure they align with your current needs and objectives.

Consider updating beneficiaries and coverage amounts as needed.

Organize Important Documents:

Gather and organize important documents, including wills, trusts, deeds, titles, insurance policies, financial statements, and legal records.

Store documents in a secure and accessible location, and inform trusted individuals of their whereabouts.
Consult with Legal and Financial Professionals:

Seek guidance from estate planning attorneys, financial advisors, and tax professionals to ensure your estate plan is comprehensive, legally sound, and optimized for your unique circumstances.

Review your estate plan regularly, at least every few years or whenever significant life events occur, to ensure it remains current and effective.

This checklist provides a framework for creating a comprehensive estate plan tailored to your individual needs and objectives. Consult with legal and financial professionals for personalized guidance and assistance throughout the estate planning process.

# Here's a basic template for a simple will:

Last Will and Testament of [Your Full Name]

I, [Your Full Name], currently residing at [Your Address], being of sound mind and disposing memory, do hereby make, publish, and declare this document to be my Last Will and Testament, hereby revoking all prior wills and codicils made by me.

Executor:
I appoint [Executor's Full Name], currently residing at [Executor's Address], to be the Executor of this Will. If [Executor's Full Name] is unable or unwilling to serve as Executor, I appoint [Alternate Executor's Full Name], currently residing at [Alternate Executor's Address], as the alternate Executor.

Debts and Expenses:
I direct my Executor to pay all my just debts, funeral expenses, and expenses of my last illness out of the assets of my estate, as soon as reasonably possible after my death.

Distribution of Property:
I give, devise, and bequeath all my property and estate, both real and personal, of whatever kind and wherever situated, to the following beneficiaries:

[Beneficiary's Full Name]: [Description of Property/Assets to be Bequeathed]
[Beneficiary's Full Name]: [Description of Property/Assets to be Bequeathed]
[Beneficiary's Full Name]: [Description of Property/Assets to be Bequeathed]
If any of the above-named beneficiaries predecease me, their share shall be distributed equally among the surviving beneficiaries.

Guardianship:

If I have minor children at the time of my death, I nominate [Guardian's Full Name], currently residing at [Guardian's Address], to be the Guardian of their persons. If [Guardian's Full Name] is unable or unwilling to serve as Guardian, I nominate [Alternate Guardian's Full Name], currently residing at [Alternate Guardian's Address], as the alternate Guardian.

Miscellaneous Provisions:

If any beneficiary named in this Will fails to survive me, their share shall be distributed equally among the surviving beneficiaries.
I authorize my Executor to sell any real property in my estate and to execute any documents necessary to effectuate such sale.
I authorize my Executor to make any distributions in cash or in kind as they deem appropriate, in their sole discretion.
IN WITNESS WHEREOF, I have hereunto set my hand and seal this [Day] day of [Month], [Year].

[Your Signature]

[Your Full Name]

Signed, sealed, published, and declared by the above-named Testator as and for their Last Will and Testament in the presence of us, who, at their request, and in their presence, and in the presence of each other, have subscribed our names as witnesses thereto.

Witnesses:

[Witness 1 Full Name]: [Witness 1 Address]
[Witness 2 Full Name]: [Witness 2 Address]
(Note: Check with local laws regarding the requirements for signing and witnessing a will.)

www.ingramcontent.com/pod-product-compliance
Lightning Source LLC
Chambersburg PA
CBHW071216240526
45470CB00018B/1880